new interchange

English for international communication
Milton Roth

Business
Companion

W0234759

CAMBRIDGE
UNIVERSITY PRESS

1

PUBLISHED BY THE PRESS SYNDICATE OF THE UNIVERSITY OF CAMBRIDGE
The Pitt Building, Trumpington Street, Cambridge, United Kingdom

CAMBRIDGE UNIVERSITY PRESS
The Edinburgh Building, Cambridge CB2 2RU, UK
40 West 20th Street, New York, NY 10011-4211, USA
477 Williamstown Road, Port Melbourne, VIC 3207, Australia
Ruiz de Alarcón 13, 28014 Madrid, Spain
Dock House, The Waterfront, Cape Town 8001, South Africa
Avenida Paulista 807 cj 2315, 01311-915 São Paulo SP, Brazil

http://www.cambridge.org

First published 2003

Printed in Hong Kong

Typeface New Century Schoolbook   *System* PageMaker®

ISBN 0-521-53649-9 pack consisting of paperback book and CD (audio)

Also available
ISBN 0-521-62881-4 Student's Book 1
ISBN 0-521-62880-6 Student's Book 1A
ISBN 0-521-62879-2 Student's Book 1B
ISBN 0-521-62878-4 Workbook 1
ISBN 0-521-62877-6 Workbook 1A
ISBN 0-521-62876-8 Workbook 1B
ISBN 0-521-62875-X Teacher's Edition 1
ISBN 0-521-62874-1 Teacher's Manual 1
ISBN 0-521-62873-3 Class Audio Cassettes 1
ISBN 0-521-62871-7 Student's Audio Cassette 1A
ISBN 0-521-62869-5 Student's Audio Cassette 1B
ISBN 0-521-62872-5 Class Audio CDs 1
ISBN 0-521-62870-9 Student's Audio CD 1A
ISBN 0-521-62868-7 Student's Audio CD 1B
ISBN 0-521-95019-8 Audio Sampler 1-3

ISBN 0-521-62867-9 Video 1 (NTSC)
ISBN 0-521-62864-4 Video Activity Book 1
ISBN 0-521-62863-6 Video Teacher's Guide 1
ISBN 0-521-63887-9 Video Sampler 1-2
ISBN 0-521-62667-6 CD-ROM (PC format)
ISBN 0-521-62666-8 CD-ROM (Mac format)
ISBN 0-521-77381-4 Lab Guide 1
ISBN 0-521-77380-6 Lab Cassettes 1
ISBN 0-521-46759-4 Placement Test (valid for New
          Interchange and Interchange)
ISBN 0-521-80575-9 Teacher Training Video (NTSC)
          with Video Manual
ISBN 0-521-62882-2 New Interchange/Passages
          Placement and Evaluation Package

Book design: Adventure House, NYC
Typesetting: Usina da Criação, São Paulo, Brazil

Illustration Credits
Drawings: pages 2, 3, 9, 21, 24, 26 and 33 by William Waitzman; pages 06 and 22 by Luciano Proença
Photograph: page 17, Jurgen Vogt/Getty Images

Author's Acknowledgements
Special thanks are due to the Cambridge University Press staff: Peter Donovan, Anne Garrett, Debbie
Goldblatt, Ben Graham, Hilary Grant, Helen Lee, Andrew Robinson, Mary Sandre, Howard Siegelman, Mary
Vaughn and all the staff in the South American Branch.

To the student

What can you learn from using _Business Companion 1_?
Business Companion 1 contains self-study exercises that allow you to practice in a professional context what you learned in **New Interchange** _Student's Book 1_. Additionally, _Business Companion 1_ presents high-interest readings from the world of international business.

When and how to use _Business Companion 1_
Do the exercises in _Business Companion 1_ after you've completed the corresponding units of **New Interchange** _Student's Book 1_ and _Workbook 1_. Be sure to follow these steps when doing the exercises:
1. Read the instructions carefully.
2. Do the exercise, then review your work.
3. Check your answers in the Answer key on page 40.
4. If you had difficulty with an exercise, wait a few days then try to do it again.

The audio CD
The audio CD in the back of this book contains recorded pronunciations of the words that appear in the _Vocabulary_ exercises, the dialogs in the _Listening_ exercises, and the questions in the _Speaking_ exercises.

Word list
A comprehensive list of business terms and key vocabulary appears on pages 34-39. To help you remember these words, space is provided for you to write definitions, notes, or translations of these words in your native language.

Answer key and audio scripts
An answer key that includes audio scripts begins on page 40. Here, you will find answers to all exercises that don't require you to provide opinions or personal information, as well as scripts of all the _Listening_ and _Speaking_ recordings that you will hear on the audio CD.

Table of contents
Business Companion 1 contains sixteen units that correspond to the units of **New Interchange** _Student's Book 1_.

1 At a company

1 Vocabulary   *Company departments and facilities*

A Sweet Chunks is a chocolate company in Salem, Massachusetts. Look at the sign in their reception area. Check (✓) the names of company departments.
(Help: Listen to the pronunciation on your audio CD. Track 2.)

Welcome to Sweet Chunks

1st floor
- ☐ Customer Service
- ☐ Order Processing
- ☐ Packaging
- ☑ Receiving
- ☐ Reception
- ☐ Shipping

2nd floor
- ☐ Accounts Payable
- ☐ Accounts Receivable
- ☐ Cafeteria
- ☐ Human Resources
- ☐ Production
- ☐ Restrooms

Have a sweet day!

Other departments in a company

Credit and Collections
Finance
Information Systems
International Trade and Customs
Personnel
Public Relations
Purchasing
Quality Control
Research and Development
Sales and Marketing

B What departments and facilities do you have in your company? Make a list.

_____   _____   _____

_____   _____   _____

2 Listening

A (Track 3) Cindy Block owns a candy store. She is at Sweet Chunks to attend meetings. Listen to her talking to the receptionist. Match the people with the departments they work in.

Name	Department
1. Charles Connor _C_	a. Order Processing
2. Brian Russell ___	b. Human Resources
3. Jennifer Smith ___	✓c. Customer Service
4. Shirley Perry ___	d. Accounts Receivable

B Write about the people at Sweet Chunks.

1. *Charles Connor is in the Customer Service Department.*

2. _____

3. _____

4. _____

Answer key and audio scripts: page 40

Language Practice *Questions with be*

(Help: Student's Book pages 4 and 6.)

A Cindy Block meets Charles Connor. He invites her for coffee in the cafeteria.
Number the sentences in the conversation in the correct order.

___ Cindy: Is she in your department?

___ Charles: Her name is Lisa Kim.

___ Charles: No, she isn't. She's in Human Resources.

___ Cindy: Where's she from?

_1_ Cindy: Who's that?

_6_ Charles: She's from New York, I think.

B Rewrite the conversation in **3A**.

Cindy: *Who's that?* _____

Charles: _____

Cindy: _____

Charles: _____

Cindy: _____

Charles: _____

C Complete the rest of the conversation.

Cindy: _____*Who's*_____ that?

Charles: _____ Brian Russell.

Cindy: _____ in Order Processing. Right?

Charles: That's right.

Cindy: And who _____ the man and the woman over there?

Are _____ in the same department?

Charles: _____ visitors, actually.

Cindy: Really? Where _____ they from?

Charles: _____ from a candy company in Georgia, I think.

Cindy: _____ are their names?

Charles: I don't know. More coffee?

Cindy: Oh, yes, please.

2 On the job

1

Vocabulary *Job titles*

A These name tags belong to people attending a business conference. Read them and underline the job titles.

(Help: Listen to the pronunciation on your audio CD. Track 4.)

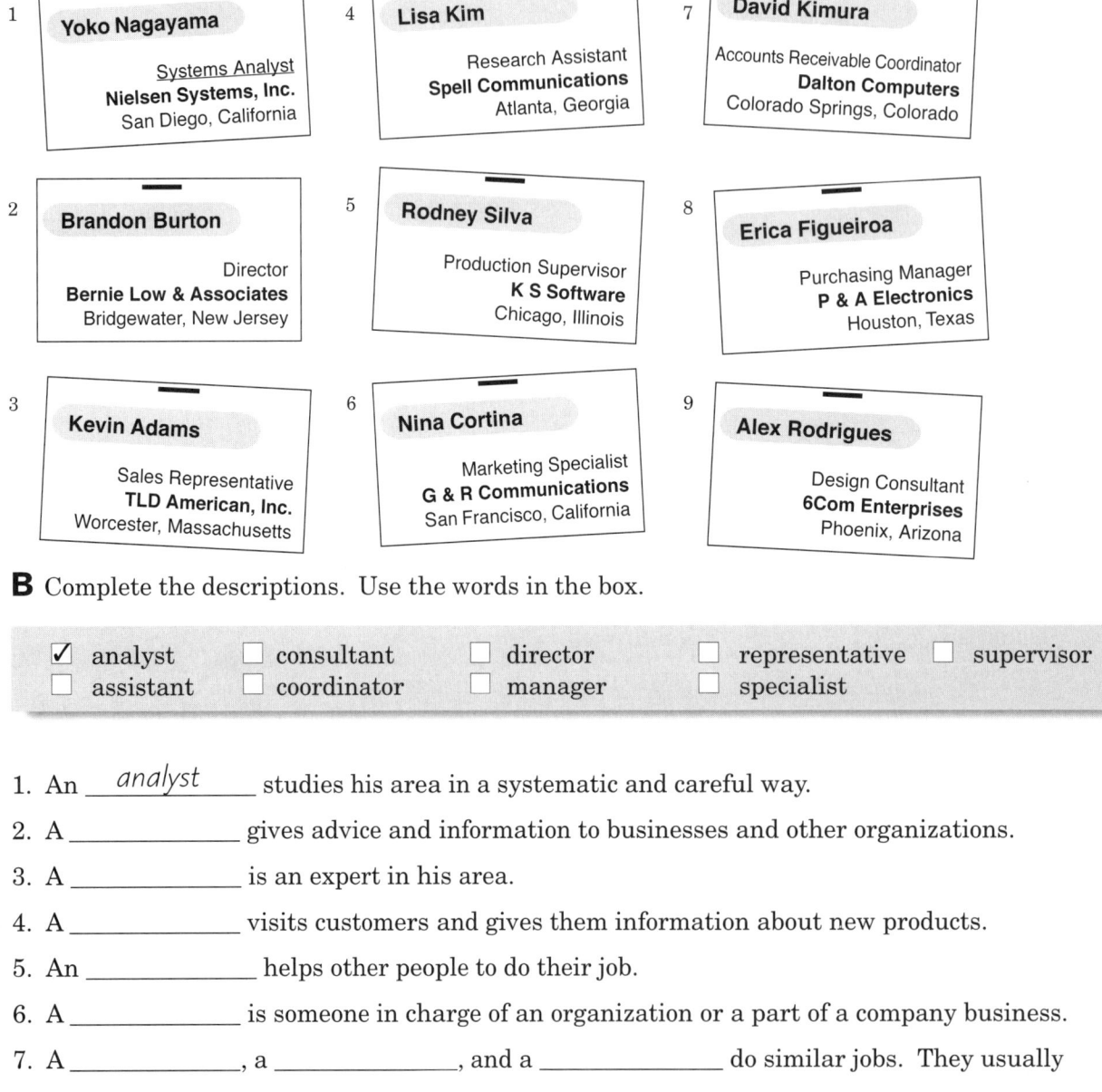

1 **Yoko Nagayama**
Systems Analyst
Nielsen Systems, Inc.
San Diego, California

2 **Brandon Burton**
Director
Bernie Low & Associates
Bridgewater, New Jersey

3 **Kevin Adams**
Sales Representative
TLD American, Inc.
Worcester, Massachusetts

4 **Lisa Kim**
Research Assistant
Spell Communications
Atlanta, Georgia

5 **Rodney Silva**
Production Supervisor
K S Software
Chicago, Illinois

6 **Nina Cortina**
Marketing Specialist
G & R Communications
San Francisco, California

7 **David Kimura**
Accounts Receivable Coordinator
Dalton Computers
Colorado Springs, Colorado

8 **Erica Figueiroa**
Purchasing Manager
P & A Electronics
Houston, Texas

9 **Alex Rodrigues**
Design Consultant
6Com Enterprises
Phoenix, Arizona

B Complete the descriptions. Use the words in the box.

☑ analyst	☐ consultant	☐ director	☐ representative	☐ supervisor
☐ assistant	☐ coordinator	☐ manager	☐ specialist	

1. An ___*analyst*___ studies his area in a systematic and careful way.

2. A _____ gives advice and information to businesses and other organizations.

3. A _____ is an expert in his area.

4. A _____ visits customers and gives them information about new products.

5. An _____ helps other people to do their job.

6. A _____ is someone in charge of an organization or a part of a company business.

7. A _____, a _____, and a _____ do similar jobs. They usually organize and monitor other people's work.

C Imagine you are attending the business conference. In your notebook, draw and complete your name tag.

Answer key and audio scripts: page 40

Language Practice *Simple present questions*

(Help: Student's Book page 10.)

A Nina Cortina meets Kevin Adams and Brandon Burton at a cocktail party during the conference. Complete the conversations with questions.

1.   Nina: Hello. I'm Nina Cortina.

   Kevin: Hello. I'm Kevin Adams. *What do you do* _____?

   Nina: I'm a marketing specialist.

   Kevin: That's interesting! _____?

   Nina: I work for G & R Communications.

   Kevin: _____?

   Nina: I like it very much. How about you?

   _____?

   Kevin: I'm a sales representative for TLD American, Inc.

2. Brandon: Hello. I'm Brandon Burton.

   Nina: Hello. I'm Nina Cortina. _____?

   Brandon: I work for Bernie Low & Associates.

   Nina: _____?

   Brandon: I'm one of the directors there.

   Nina: Really! That's interesting! _____?

   Brandon: I love it!

B Look at Alex Rodrigues's name tag. Complete the questions.

1. A: What _____?

   B: He's a design consultant.

2. A: Where _____?

   B: He works for 6Com Enterprises.

3. A: _____ from Chicago?

   B: No, he isn't. He's from Phoenix.

> ———
> **Alex Rodrigues**
>
> Design Consultant
> **6Com Enterprises**
> Phoenix, Arizona

---

3 **Speaking**

((•)) (Track 5) You meet Nina Cortina at the cocktail party. Answer her questions aloud.

> *Hi! I'm Nina Cortina.*
> *What's your name?*

3 Buying equipment

1 Reading

A Erica Figueroa, Purchasing Manager at P & A Electronics, needs to buy a computer and a fax machine for her department. She is looking at some ads in a newspaper. Match them with Erica's comments.

1 *c*

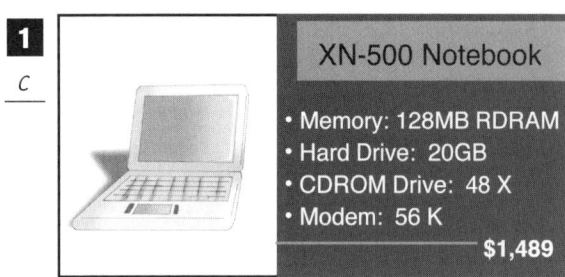

XN-500 Notebook
- Memory: 128MB RDRAM
- Hard Drive: 20GB
- CDROM Drive: 48 X
- Modem: 56 K

$1,489

2

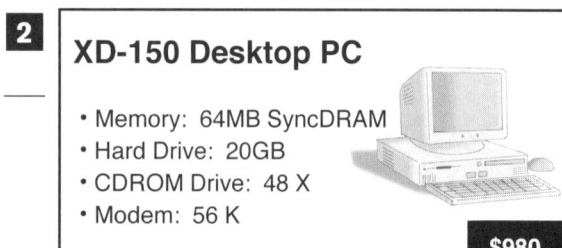

XD-150 Desktop PC
- Memory: 64MB SyncDRAM
- Hard Drive: 20GB
- CDROM Drive: 48 X
- Modem: 56 K

$980

3

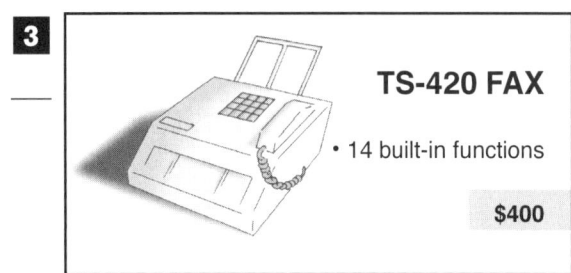

TS-420 FAX
- 14 built-in functions

$400

4

T-600 FAX
- Answering Machine
- 32 built-in functions
- Accepts documents of up to 50 pages

$450

a. "I like this one better. It has eighteen more functions than the other one and it has an answering machine, too. Of course, it's more expensive but the price is still reasonable. The difference is only $50. Also, it looks more modern and more sophisticated."

b. "I prefer this one. It's cheaper than the other one. And it is a great value at less than a $1,000. It has half the memory, but we only need to use the word processor. Sixty-four megabytes is enough for that."

c. "Of course this one is smaller and lighter, but look at the price! Almost fifteen hundred dollars. That's pretty expensive. Also, we really need a desktop model, not a laptop."

d. "This one is cheaper, but it doesn't have an answering machine. It's bigger, too, and it looks more complicated. I don't really like it at all."

B Read Erica's comments again. Which two items do you think she will buy? Which ones would *you* buy? Complete the sentences with the item numbers.

1. I think Erica will buy items ____ and ____.

2. I would buy items ____ and ____.

Answer key and audio scripts: page 40

Writing *An e-mail message*

(Help: Preferences and comparisons. Student's Book page 18.)

A Erica wants to buy a new photocopier, too. She asks a colleague for her opinion. Complete Erica's e-mail. Use the words in the box.

☐ cheaper	✓ faster	☐ larger	☐ than	☐ more

				New photocopier				
File	Edit	View	Insert	Format	Tools	Message	Help	
Send	Cut	Copy	Paste	Undo	Attachment			

From	Erica Figueroa
Date	Wednesday, August 1st
To	Juliet Carter
Subject	New photocopier

Dear Juliet,

We're thinking of buying a new copier for our department. Please have a look at the ads below. I prefer the Super FX Copier. It's __*faster*__ (thirteen copies per minute!), and it makes legal and letter size copies. The sheet cassette is _____, too. Of course, it's much _____ expensive _____ the FX but the copies are _____. What do you think?

Many thanks.

Erica

FX Copier
• 4 Copies Per Minute
• 30 Seconds Warm-up
  Time
• Legal Size Copy
• 100 Sheet Cassette
• Approximate cost per
  copy: 6.5 cents
Our price: $995

Super FX Copier
• 13 Copies Per Minute
• 0 Second Warm-up Time
• Letter and Legal Size Copy
• Reduction & Enlargement from
  70% to 200%.
• 500 Sheet Cassette
• Approximate cost per copy:
  4 cents
Our price: $1795

B You need to buy a new printer for your department. Look at the ads below. In your notebook, write an e-mail to the person in charge of buying equipment in your company. Use Erica's e-mail as a model.

X1500 Laser Printer
• 8 Pages Per Minute
• 100 Sheet Paper Capacity
• 600X600 dpi Resolution
• Approximate cost per print:
  2 cents
Our price: $375

NZ Laser Printer 8500
• 24 Pages Per Minute
• 1000 Sheet Paper Capacity
• 600X600 dpi Resolution
• Approximate cost per print:
  1 cent
Our price: $2799

Business visitors

1

Vocabulary *Hotels and entertainment*

The Visitor Profile below is a questionnaire for business visitors to K S Software in New York. Read it and underline the words that are new for you.
(Help: Listen to the pronunciation on your audio CD. Track 6.)

K S Software
New York Branch

VISITOR PROFILE

Dear _____,

Please take a minute to fill out this questionnaire and fax it to us a week before your arrival in New York. It will help us plan your visit according to your needs.

Hotel Accommodations

1 What kind of hotels do you prefer?
- ☐ three-star
- ☐ four-star
- ☑ five-star

2 Which facilities do you expect to find in your hotel?
- ☐ a swimming pool
- ☐ a fitness center
- ☐ a sauna

3 What kind of room do you prefer?
- ☐ standard   ☐ deluxe
- ☐ smoking   ☐ non-smoking

4 Which facilities do you expect to find in your room?
- ☐ a safe   ☐ air conditioning
- ☐ a fax   ☐ an Internet connection

Food preferences

5 What kind of food do you like?
- ☐ international food
- ☐ ethnic food
- ☐ vegetarian food

Entertainment

6 When you have some free time on a trip, what do you like to do?
- ☐ go sightseeing
- ☐ go shopping
- ☐ stay in and rest
- ☐ go out to dinner or see a show

Thanks for answering this questionnaire. We are all looking forward to your visit.

2

Listening

A (Track 7) Rodney Silva, from K S Software in Chicago, is going to visit his company's New York branch. Listen to him completing the Visitor Profile. Check (✓) his answers.

B Imagine you are going to visit K S Software in New York. How would you answer the questions in the Visitor Profile? Circle your choices.

Answer key and audio scripts: page 41

3 Language Practice *Questions with do*

(Help: Student's Book page 21.)

A Arrange these words to make questions.

1. hotels prefer he does kind what of
   *What kind of hotels does he prefer*_____?

2. he shopping like does
   _____?

3. time he have any does free
   _____?

4. do does evenings he in like the to what
   _____?

5. food like he does international
   _____?

B Two K S Software employees in New York are looking at Rodney Silva's Visitor Profile. Use the questions in **3A** to complete their conversation.

A: *What kind of hotels does he prefer*_____?

B: He likes five-star hotels.

A: Let's put him up at the Plaza. What about food preferences?
   _____?

B: Well, in fact, he likes all kinds of food.

A: Oh good. _____?

B: He's free all day on Friday.

A: And _____?

B: No, he doesn't like shopping, but he enjoys sightseeing.

A: Let's take him on a river cruise around Manhattan Island.

B: That's a good idea.

A: And _____?

B: Not much, really. He likes to stay in and rest.

---

4 Speaking

(Track 8) You meet a business colleague from abroad.
Answer his questions aloud.

> When you have some free time on a business trip, what do you like to do?

Answer key and audio scripts: page 41

5 Families in business

A Look at the names of famous American families. Guess which families are in the world of business. Check (✓) their names.

☐ Baldwin	☐ Jackson	☐ Kennedy	☐ Mars
✓ Campbell	☐ Johnson	☐ Lauder	☐ Sheen

B (Track 9) Listen to information about the business families.
Check your answers to **1A**.

C Listen again. Complete the chart.
(Help: Glossary page 38.)

A. Family	B. Starting date	C. Line of business	D. Successful product
Campbell	1869		condensed soup
		flooring	floor wax
		candy-making	
	1946		perfumes

D Complete the sentences. Use information from **1C**.
(Grammar note: Notice the use of the simple present to talk about the past.)

1. In <u>1869</u> Joseph Campbell and Abraham Anderson start <u>a food business.</u>
   <u>Their most successful product is condensed soup.</u>

2. In _____ Samuel Curtis Johnson starts _____

   _____

3. In _____ Frank C. Mars and his wife _____

   _____

4. In _____ Estee Lauder's uncle _____

   _____

Answer key and audio scripts: page 41

Writing *A memo*

(Help: Determiners. Student's Book page 32.)

A Spell Communications is doing a survey to find out more about its employees and their families. Look at the heading of the memo below and answer the questions.

1. Who is the memo for? *The board of directors.*

2. Who is sending it? _____

3. What is the date of the memo? _____

4. What is the memo about? _____

Spell Communications
635 Hansell Street
Atlanta, Georgia
USA 30306

memo

To: The board of directors   **Date**: Thursday, July 31ˢᵗ
From: Lisa Kim   **Subject**: Employee Profile Survey
        Research Assistant

****

This is a summary of the Employee Profile Survey findings. The results include all employees who are not in management positions, a total of 59.

Age and gender

*Nearly all* employees (98%) are between 20 and 30 years old. Just over _____ of them (51%) are male.

Qualifications

_____ employees (80%) have undergraduate degrees.

_____ (13%) have higher degrees.

Marital status and family

_____ (60%) are married. Out of these, 80% have no children, _____ (15%) have one child and _____ (5%) have two children. _____ has more than two children.

B Read the memo and complete it. Use the words in the box.
(More than one answer is possible.)

☐ a few	☐ many	☑ nearly all	☐ some
☐ half	☐ most	☐ no one	☐ very few

C In your notebook, list the names of the people that work in your department. Find out about (or guess!) their age, qualifications, marital status and family. Then write a memo summarizing the results of your "survey." Use Lisa's memo as a model.

6 Managing time

1 Reading

A Read the texts on how to manage your time. Choose a title for each text. Write the letters in the boxes.

a. Keep mind and body healthy. ☑
b. Efficiency over perfection. ☐
c. Make it simple. ☐
d. Finish what you started. ☐
e. The sooner, the better. ☐
f. Think before you act. ☐

☐ When a new activity or responsibility is too complicated, divide it into smaller parts or steps. This way, something very complicated can become easier and more manageable.

_____

---

a To make the most of your time, you need to be well mentally and physically. This is why many companies now have gyms for their staff. Make sure you exercise at least three times a week.

_____

☐ Many people never plan their day. Before you start working, it is important to spend some time organizing your activities for the day. This helps you save a lot of time.

_____

☐ Don't start a new activity until you finish what you're doing. It's very easy to start a hundred different things and not finish any of them! This is inefficient and stressful.

_____

☐ Always try to answer letters and e-mail messages immediately after you read them. If you leave them for later you spend more time. Why? Because you have to read them again to answer them!

_____

☐ Don't pay too much attention to small details. For example, it is not necessary to correct an internal memo five or six times to make it complete and correct in every way. People who try to be perfect all the time never do anything on time!

_____

B Read the texts again. What do you think of the suggestions? Write your opinion on the lines at the bottom of the texts. Use expressions from the box.

| I agree. | I agree only in part. | I don't agree at all. | I don't really know. |

C Write one more suggestion for managing time effectively.

_____

_____

Answer key and audio scripts: page 41

2 **Language Practice** *Adverbs of frequency and questions with how*

(Help: Student's Book pages 35 and 38.)

A Match the phrases in **A** and **B** to make questions.

A	B
1. How much time do you _f_	**a.** personal calls at work?
2. How often do you ____	**b.** complicated activities?
3. How good are you ____	**c.** letters and e-mail messages immediately?
4. Do you always try to answer ____	**d.** at planning your day?
5. Do you ever make ____	**e.** exercise at the company gym?
6. How well do you manage ____	✓**f.** spend correcting memos?

B Complete with the appropriate questions from **2A**.

1. A: *How much time do you spend correcting memos* ?

   B: Very little. I hardly ever correct internal documents more than once.

2. A: _____?

   B: No. I never phone my friends from work.

3. A: _____?

   B: Pretty well, I think. I usually try to make complicated things simple.

4. A: _____?

   B: Yes. I almost always reply at once.

5. A: _____?

   B: Once a week only. I'm a real couch potato!

6. A: _____?

   B: Quite good, actually. I almost always spend ten or fifteen minutes organizing
   things before I start work.

C In your notebook, write *your own* answers to the questions in **2B**.

---

3 **Speaking**

(Track 10) A colleague asks you how you manage your time. Answer her
questions aloud.

> Are you good at
> managing your time?

7 Company finances

1 **Vocabulary** *Finances*

Study P & A Electronics' financial statements. Then match the words in the box with their definitions.

(Help: Listen to the pronunciation on your audio CD. Track 11.)

P & A Electronics	
Financial Statement	1ˢᵗ Quarter
Revenue	$5,102,000
Total Costs	$3,571,400
– Production Costs	$1,714,272
– Overhead	$1,212,128
– Taxes	$645,000
Profit	$1,530,600
Profit Margin	30%

P & A Electronics	
Financial Statement	2ⁿᵈ Quarter
Revenue	$5,000,000
Total Costs	$3,992,613
– Production Costs	$1,913,027
– Overhead	$1,334,586
– Taxes	$745,000
Profit	$1,007,387
Profit Margin	20%

Words	Definitions
1. revenue __g__	a. A percentage that shows how well the company is doing.
2. total costs ____	b. Money the company makes.
3. production costs ____	c. Money paid to the government.
4. overhead ____	d. All the costs together.
5. taxes ____	e. Rent, salaries, electricity, phone bills, office supplies, etc.
6. profit ____	f. The cost of making products.
7. profit margin ____	✓ g. Total money the company receives.

2 **Language Practice** *Past tense*

(Help: Student's Book pages 41 and 43.)

Eileen Wilkins, Finance Manager at P & A Electronics, is talking to a financial consultant. Complete the conversation.

Consultant: How much profit ___did___ you ___make___ (make) in the first quarter?

Eileen: About $1,530,000.

Consultant: And what _____ (be) your profit margin?

Eileen: It was thirty percent. But the second quarter _____ (not be) very good.

Consultant: Really? Why?

Eileen: Our production costs _____ (be) higher and overhead and taxes _____ (go) up, too.

Consultant: _____ your profit margin _____ (go) down?

Eileen: Yes. It _____ (be) twenty percent.

Answer key and audio scripts: page 42

A Eileen Wilkins is calling a meeting to discuss the financial situation at P & A Electronics. Read her memo and number the paragraphs in the correct order.

P & A Electronics
1600 North Street
Houston, Texas
USA 77088

memo

To: All managers   **Date**:   Thursday, July 31ˢᵗ
From: Eileen Wilkins   **Subject**: Financial situation

Strictly Confidential
****

_____ I would like to call a meeting for three o'clock in the afternoon on August 3ʳᵈ so that we can discuss the situation and brainstorm possible solutions.

_*1*_ As you can see from the financial statements on the previous page, the company's performance in the second quarter of the year was far from satisfactory. Although our revenue was practically the same as in the first quarter, our profits were down.

_____ There are two crucial questions we need to discuss at the meeting: how to reduce production costs and how to reduce overhead. Please bring suggestions and creative ideas.

_____ Why did this happen? First of all, in the second quarter we spent about $200,000 more on production than in the first quarter. Secondly, our overhead went up by about ten percent. Finally, there was a tax increase which, in our case, meant $100,000 more on taxes. In short, all of our costs went up.

B Read the memo again. Check (✓) True or False.

		True	False
1.	Eileen Wilkins says the revenue in the second quarter was lower than in the first quarter.	☐	✓
2.	She doesn't know why the company's profits were lower in the second quarter.	☐	☐
3.	She is worried about the company at the moment.	☐	☐
4.	She is calling a meeting to discuss taxes.	☐	☐
5.	She's not interested in the other managers' opinions.	☐	☐

8 Company facilities

1 Vocabulary Facilities

What facilities do the sentences describe? Find the names in the box and write them
in the correct spaces.
(Help: Listen to the pronunciation on your audio CD. Track 12.)

☐ conference room   ☐ mailroom   ☐ showroom
☐ copy room   ☐ production line   ☐ stockroom
☐ lunch room   ☑ reception   ☐ visitor center

1. _____reception_____ : There is a person at a desk to welcome visitors.

2. _____ : There is a coffee-maker, a refrigerator, and a microwave here.

3. _____ : Here, people can see samples of the company's products.

4. _____ : There are several machines here and it can be very noisy.

5. _____ : People have meetings here.

6. _____ : There are comfortable chairs, a sofa, and a TV here.

7. _____ : Clerks send out products from this room.

8. _____ : There are several photocopiers in this room.

9. _____ : There are shelves to keep supplies and products organized here.

2 Listening

A (Track 13) Listen to three people talk about where they work. Number the floor plans.

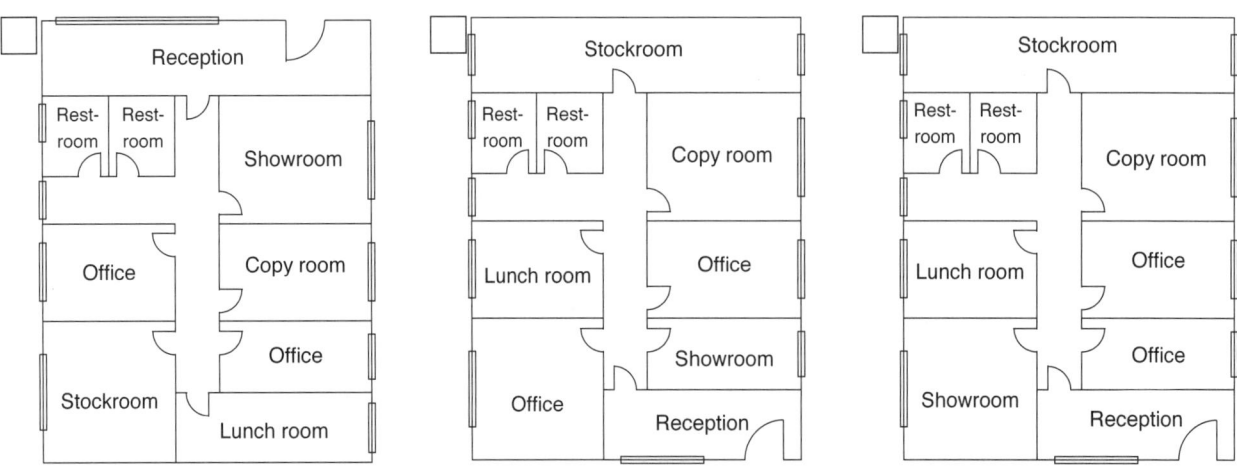

B In your notebook, draw a simple floor plan of your company's office site. Then write
a description of it.

16

Answer key and audio scripts: page 42

Language Practice   *There is, there are, how much, how many*

(Help: Student's Book pages 47 and 50.)

A Look at plan 1 in **2A**. Correct the sentences.

1. There's a mailroom.
   There isn't a mailroom.

2. There isn't a lunch room.

   _____

3. There's a visitor center.

   _____

4. There aren't any offices.

   _____

5. There are three conference rooms.

   _____

B Look at plan 1 in **2A** again.   Then look at the answers.   What are the questions?

1. *Is there a conference room* _____?

   No, there isn't.

2. _____?

   Yes, there is.   It's next to the stockroom.

3. _____?

   Yes, there are two.   One is big and the other one small.

4. _____?

   There are two.   They're very small.

5. _____?

   There's a lot of space in the stockroom.

---

4 **Speaking**

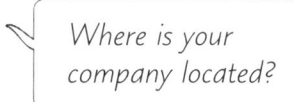 (Track 14) Answer the questions about your company's office site aloud.

> Where is your
> company located?

9 Promoting staff

1 Vocabulary *Personal qualities*

A Complete the word map with the opposites of the words on the list.
(Help: Listen to the pronunciation on your audio CD. Track 15.)

committed ✓
competent
friendly
hardworking
honest
loyal
optimistic
organized
punctual
responsible
sensitive
sympathetic

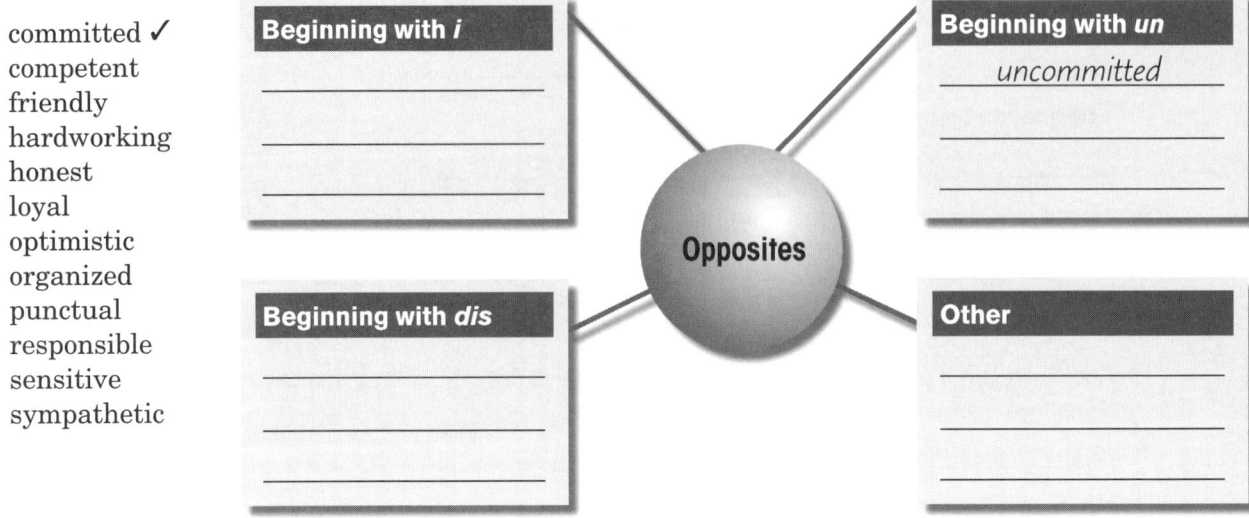

Beginning with *i*
_____
_____
_____

Beginning with *un*
uncommitted
_____
_____

Opposites

Beginning with *dis*
_____
_____
_____

Other
_____
_____
_____

B How do you see yourself? Write a sentence.

I think I'm sensitive, competent, and friendly, but I'm not very punctual.

_____

2 Listening

A (Track 16) John Dalton and Liz Holmes, from Dalton Computers, are talking about promoting some employees. Listen and check (✓) the candidates' qualities.

Names	Candidates' qualities		
Pam Carson	☐ committed	✓ competent	☐ responsible
Henry Crane	☐ friendly	☐ honest	☐ sensitive
Meg Trent	☐ punctual	☐ loyal	☐ optimistic

B Listen again. Check(✓) True or False.

	True	False
1. Pam Carson is not very sympathetic.	✓	☐
2. Henry Crane is a bit disorganized.	☐	☐
3. Meg Trent is very friendly.	☐	☐

Answer key and audio scripts: pages 42 and 43

3 **Writing** *An e-mail message*

(Help: Modifiers with participles and prepositions. Student's Book page 58.)

A Liz Holmes writes an e-mail message to John Dalton about two other candidates for promotion. Complete her message with these comments.

1. She plans her activities carefully and always finishes on time.
2. Everybody likes her a lot.
3. She never arrives late to work or to a meeting.
4. She's the one working late every evening.

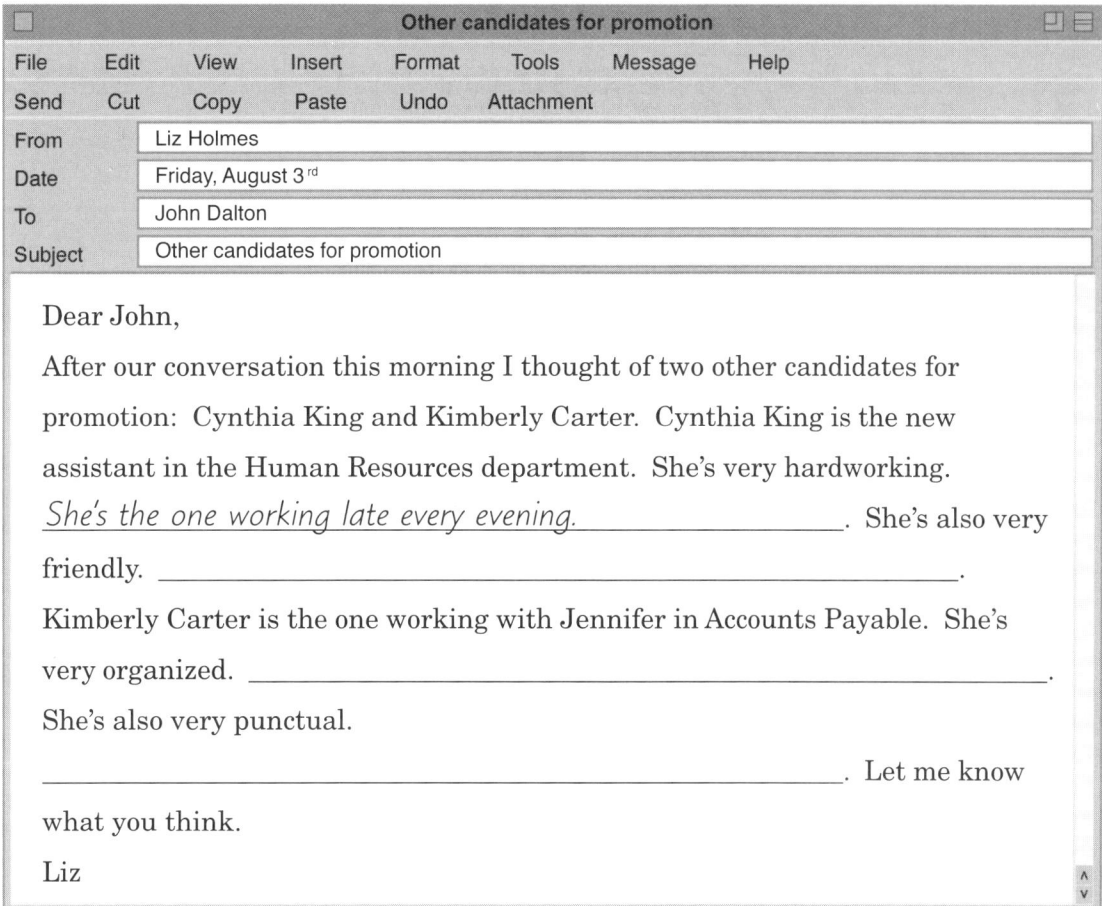

Other candidates for promotion

| File | Edit | View | Insert | Format | Tools | Message | Help |

| Send | Cut | Copy | Paste | Undo | Attachment |

From	Liz Holmes
Date	Friday, August 3 rd
To	John Dalton
Subject	Other candidates for promotion

Dear John,

After our conversation this morning I thought of two other candidates for
promotion: Cynthia King and Kimberly Carter. Cynthia King is the new
assistant in the Human Resources department. She's very hardworking.
She's the one working late every evening. _____. She's also very
friendly. _____.
Kimberly Carter is the one working with Jennifer in Accounts Payable. She's
very organized. _____.
She's also very punctual.
_____. Let me know
what you think.

Liz

B Think of two candidates for promotion in your company. Complete the chart.

Name	Department	Qualities	Comment

C In your notebook, write an e-mail to your boss recommending the candidates you chose in **3B**. Use Liz's e-mail as a model.

10 Delegating tasks

1 **Vocabulary** *Common office tasks*

(Help: Listen to the pronunciation on your audio CD. Track 17.)

A Read the phrases. Which ones have the same meaning? Which ones have different meanings? Check (✓) Same or Different.

Common office tasks		Same	Different
1. Place an order.	Process an order.	☐	✓
2. Contact customers.	Get in touch with customers.	☐	☐
3. Write a report.	File a report.	☐	☐
4. Schedule a meeting.	Attend a meeting.	☐	☐
5. Make an appointment.	Cancel an appointment.	☐	☐
6. Update customer records.	Add new customer records.	☐	☐
7. Check e-mail messages.	Reply to e-mail messages.	☐	☐

B Underline the verbs in the phrases above. Which ones are irregular?

C Complete the job description. Use verbs from **1B**.

JOB DESCRIPTION

Position: Marketing Assistant

Main responsibilities

1. _____*Add*_____ new customer records to our database and _____ existing ones when necessary.

2. _____ customer's orders as soon as we receive them.

3. _____ e-mail messages every half hour.

4. _____ customers and _____ appointments with them.

Other responsibilities

5. _____ reports and other important documents the Marketing Manager sends or receives.

6. _____ general staff meetings once a month.

D In your notebook, write three things you have done at work this week.

I've attended three meetings.

Answer key and audio scripts: page 43

2 **Language Practice** *Present perfect and past tense*
(Help: Student's Book pages 61 and 62.)

Brandon Burton, Director at Bernie Low & Associates, is on a trip. He left a list of tasks for his assistant. He is now talking to his assistant on the phone. Complete the conversation.

Brandon: *Have you scheduled* _____
(you/schedule) the meeting with Mr. Miles yet?

Assistant: I'm afraid not. Mr. Miles is on vacation this week. I'll call him again on Monday.

Brandon: OK. _____
(you/already/contact) the lawyer about the new contract?

Assistant: Yes. I _____
(call) him an hour ago. He's working on it.
I _____ (ask) him to phone us when it's ready.

Brandon: Fine. _____
(have) time to process the Crandon order?

Assistant: Yes and I _____
(also/update) several customer records.

Brandon: Great! Well, thanks for doing all that.

---

3 **Speaking**

A Imagine you are a marketing assistant. Your manager is on a trip. She left you some tasks to do. You've done only two! Check (✓) them. Then think of the reasons why you haven't done the other tasks.

> *While I'm away please...*
>
> • *Check e-mail.* ☐
> • *Process orders.* ☐
> • *Add new customer records. Friday afternoon is a good time for this.* ☐
> • *Contact managers about the meeting next week.* ☐
> • *File all the documents on my desk.* ☐
> • *Take my kids to the soccer game on Saturday.* ☐

B (Track 18) It's Monday morning. Your manager calls you. Answer her questions aloud. Give reasons for the tasks you haven't done.

> *Have you checked the e-mail?*

11 Famous business centers

1 Reading

A Look at the names of the places described in the text. What do you know about them? In your notebook, make notes.

Avenida Paulista

Avenida Paulista is one of the most important business centers in South America. Until the 1950's, it used to be mainly a residential area famous for its luxurious mansions. Gradually, because of its convenient location, many businesses started moving to this area. Today, this avenue is one of Brazil's landmarks with some of the tallest skyscrapers in the country. When visiting the area, make sure you take a look at the FIESP building.

Wall Street

In colonial times, when the Dutch governed New York, they built a wall to separate themselves from the Native Americans and the British. This is what gave Wall Street its present name. In 1792, the Stock Exchange was opened and transformed this area into one of the most renowned business centers in the world. The Federal Reserve Bank (the Fed) is located here, too. The Fed is open to the public. Tours are free of charge, but you must be at least 16 years old to enter.

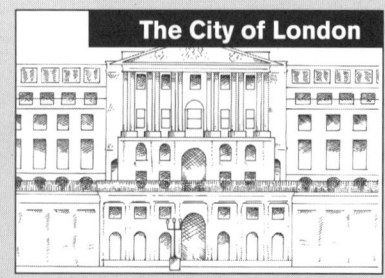

The City of London

This "city" is in fact a county of London. Some people call it the "Square Mile" because of its size. Many historic buildings stand here. St. Paul's Cathedral, Guildhall and Mansion House are some examples. The financial district is also here and it includes buildings such as the Bank of England, the Royal Exchange and the Stock Exchange. One of the few modern buildings you can visit is the Gherkin. It has 41 floors and is the tallest building in the area.

B Read the descriptions. Have you learned anything new about the places?

C Read the descriptions again. Check (✓) True or False.

	True	False
1. There are many mansions but no skyscrapers on Avenida Paulista.	☐	☑
2. An advantage of Avenida Paulista is its location.	☐	☐
3. In colonial times there was a wall where Wall Street is.	☐	☐
4. If you're 14, you can't go on a tour of the Fed.	☐	☐
5. There are some very old buildings in the City of London.	☐	☐
6. The Gherkin is one of the oldest buildings in the area.	☐	☐

Answer key and audio scripts: page 43

Language Practice *Modal verbs can and should*

(Help: Student's Book page 69.)

A Henry is visiting New York for the first time. His friend Debbie is a New Yorker. Read their conversation and study the underlined sentences. Which ones ask for or give suggestions? Check (✓) them.

Henry: Can you tell me a little about Wall Street?

Debbie: Sure, what do you want to know?

Henry: <u>Well, what places should I visit?</u> ✓

Debbie: <u>You should visit the Fed.</u> ☐

Henry: What's that?

Debbie: The Federal Reserve Bank. <u>It's a really exciting place!</u> ☐

Henry: <u>Is that where they keep the gold?</u> ☐

Debbie: Exactly. <u>And you shouldn't miss the New York Stock Exchange.</u> ☐
It's a beautiful building.

Henry: <u>Can I go inside it?</u> ☐

Debbie: Sure. It's open to the public. <u>Ask for visiting hours at your hotel.</u> ☐

Henry: Great. Thanks for all the suggestions.

Debbie: No problem. By the way, did you say you were buying me lunch today?

B Think of some interesting places in your city. Complete the chart.

Place	Comment
Sugar Loaf Mountain	It's a fascinating place.

Useful adjectives

attractive	interesting
beautiful	large
best	modern
exciting	old
famous	pretty
fascinating	relaxing
great	terrific
huge	unique
incredible	wonderful

C Now write a few suggestions for a visitor to your city.

1. You should *visit Sugar Loaf Mountain. It's a fascinating place.*

2. You shouldn't _____

3. You can _____

4. You shouldn't _____

5. You can also _____

6. Finally, you should _____

Useful verbs

visit
see
go
miss
spend
try

12 Health at work

1 Listening

A (Track 19) Look at the illustrations of health problems. Then listen to people talking about health problems at work. Match the information in columns A, B, and C.

A Name   *B Health problem*   *C Reason*

Sue   eye strain   lifts heavy things
Kate   hearing loss   looks at a computer screen all day
Chris   RSI (repetitive strain injury)   works in a noisy place
Ken   stress   types many hours a day
Bob   back trouble   works too much

B In your notebook, use the information in **1A** to write about the people's problems.

Sue suffers from hearing loss because she works in a noisy place.

2 Language Practice   *Infinitive complements and modal verbs*
(Help: Student's Book pages 73 and 75.)

What advice would you give to people suffering from these problems? Use the ideas in the box to complete the sentences.

1. Eye strain: I suggest *you use some eye drops.* _____

2. Back trouble: You should _____

3. RSI: It's important _____

4. Stress: Try _____

5. Hearing loss: It's a good idea _____

Suggestions

- Take short breaks every hour.
- Use some eye drops.
- Use ear plugs.
- Exercise two or three times a week.
- Avoid lifting heavy things.

Answer key and audio scripts: pages 43 and 44

3 **Writing** *A notice in the workplace*

(Help: Infinitive complements and modal verbs. Student's Book pages 73 and 75.)

A Read the notice in the lunch room of a small factory. Match the health complaints with the recommendations.

| 1. the flu | 2. headaches | 3. bad posture | 4. stress | 5. RSI | 6. head injuries |

Better safe than sorry!

Here are some tips for keeping healthy at work:

[ ] It's a good idea to wear your helmet at all times.

[1] It's important that all employees take a flu shot.

[ ] If you are a computer operator, you should take a five-minute break every hour.

[ ] Try to sit with your knees lower than your hips.

[ ] You should relieve pressure on your neck by doing stretching exercises.

[ ] Finally, you should try our new gym. It's free, it's fun, and it's relaxing!

B Think of some common health complaints at your workplace. Complete the notice.

Better safe than sorry!

Here are some tips for keeping healthy at work:

_____

_____

_____

_____

_____

_____

---

4 **Speaking**

(Track 20) What advice do you have for other common health complaints? Answer the questions aloud.

> *What do you suggest for sore muscles?*

Answer key and audio scripts: page 44

13 Business meals

1

Listening

A  (Track 21) Kevin Adams, a sales representative, took an important customer to dinner last night. Listen to Kevin talking to his manager about the dinner. Check (✓) the correct boxes.

Who...	Kevin	The customer
1. made a reservation at a Japanese restaurant?	✓	☐
2. hates Japanese food?	☐	☐
3. tried to talk business before the meal?	☐	☐
4. can't stand talking business before a meal?	☐	☐
5. tried to pay for dinner?	☐	☐
6. actually paid for dinner?	☐	☐
7. sang with the mariachis?	☐	☐

B Listen again. Kevin was not pleased with the dinner. Give two possible reasons.

1. _____

2. _____

C What is acceptable at a business lunch or dinner? What is *not* acceptable?
Check (✓) the tips that you don't agree with. Then write two more tips of your own.

Tips for a Successful Business Lunch or Dinner

1. Ask your guest what kind of food he or she likes. ☐

2. Always let your guest order first. ☐

3. Ask your guest to choose only cheap dishes. ☐

4. Suggest a good dish if you see it on the menu. ☐

5. Try not to talk business until after you have ordered. ☐

6. Never let your guest pay for the meal. ☐

7. Talk to your guest about your personal problems. ☐

8. _____

9. _____

Answer key and audio scripts: page 44

Language Practice *Modal verbs would and will; so, too, neither, either*
(Help: Student's Book pages 83 and 81.)

A Kevin is having a business lunch with another customer, Mr. Stock. Complete the conversation. Use the questions in the box.

☐ How about you, sir?   ☐ What would you like to order?
☑ May I take your order?   ☐ Would you like anything else?
☐ What kind of salad would you like?   ☐ Would you like anything to drink?

Waiter: *May I take your order*_____?

Kevin: Yes, please. I'd like the grilled salmon and a salad.

Waiter: _____?

Kevin: I think I'll have a mixed green salad.

Waiter: _____?

Kevin: I'll just have mineral water.

Waiter: _____?

_____?

Mr. Stock: I'd like the roast chicken with a tossed salad and

a soda, please.

Waiter: _____?

Mr. Stock: No, thank you. That will be all.

B Read the conversation in **2A** again. What does Kevin do wrong this time?
Check (✓) the correct answer.

☐ He talks business before ordering.   ☐ He doesn't let the guest order first.

C Respond to the statements giving your opinion. Use *so*, *too*, *neither*, and *either*
where appropriate.

1. I like going out to dinner with customers. *So do I.*_____

2. I'm not crazy about socializing with customers. _____

3. I don't enjoy talking business over a meal. _____

4. I'm crazy about Japanese food. _____

5. I can't stand noisy restaurants. _____

6. I always try to go to quiet restaurants for business dinners. _____

Answer key and audio scripts: page 44

Business superlatives

1 Reading

A How well-known are these businesses in your country? Number them from
0 (=**not well-known**) to 6 (=**well-known**).

- [ ] Citigroup
- [ ] General Electric
- [ ] Indian Railways
- [ ] Toys "R" Us
- [ ] Walmart
- [ ] West Edmonton Mall

LARGEST OF THE LARGE

When it comes to companies, the largest of the large is General Electric Co. This gigantic American operation can generate profits of over $10 billion a year. In 1999, for example, their profits reached a total of $10.7 billion. One of the reasons behind GE's success is that, over the years, they have managed to diversify their products. You can buy anything from a GE refrigerator for your home to a GE turbine engine for a plane!

The company with the most employees in the world is Indian Railways. In 1997 this company was providing jobs for over 1.5 million people. That is more than five times the population of Iceland and more than three times the population of Luxembourg!

In the highly-competitive world of banking, no one is bigger than Citigroup, with a market capitalization of $207.1 billion in May 2000. Citigroup has been ranked by different organizations as "the best bank," "one of the 100 best companies for working mothers," and "the top foreign exchange bank."

In 1962, Sam Walton founded Walmart in Arkansas, USA. Some four decades later, this company has a total revenue of about $165 million, over 4,000 outlets in 10 different countries, and over a million employees. All of this makes Walmart the world's largest retailer. In 2000, Walmart was named the 5th most admired company in America by Fortune magazine.

Charles Lazarus started a business focussing on kids and their needs in Paramus, New Jersey, in 1948. At that time, he could hardly imagine that Toys "R" Us would turn into an $11 billion dollar business and become the world's largest toy retailer with 1,552 stores in twenty-seven countries.

Do you want to go on a shopping spree? Do you want to visit the most expensive shopping complex in the world? Then the West Edmonton Mall in Alberta, Canada, is the place to go. This huge complex opened in 1981 and has a total area of 1,584,000 square feet. There are more than 800 businesses in the complex, including eleven major department stores. The mall also has the world's biggest parking lot, with 20,000 parking spaces.

B According to the article, which businesses are the following true about?
Check (✓) the correct boxes.

	GE	Indian Railways	Citi-group	Walmart	Toys "R" Us	WE Mall
1. This company makes products for very young people.	☐	☐	☐	☐	✓	☐
2. This is the largest employer in the world.	☐	☐	☐	☐	☐	☐
3. This is *not* the largest employer in the world, but it gives jobs to over 1,000,000 people.	☐	☐	☐	☐	☐	☐
4. No other company earns larger profits.	☐	☐	☐	☐	☐	☐
5. Here you can shop at many department stores.	☐	☐	☐	☐	☐	☐
6. Some people think there is no better bank.	☐	☐	☐	☐	☐	☐

Answer key and audio scripts: page 44

Language Practice   *Comparisons with adjectives*
(Help: Student's Book page 87.)

A Write sentences. Use the cues in parentheses.

1. *The highest paid CEO in the world is Charles B. Wang.*

   (high paid / CEO / world / Charles B. Wang)

2. _____

   (low paid / CEO / world / Steve Jobs)

3. _____

   (rich investor / world / Warren Buffet)

4. _____

   (Hoshi Ryokan in Japan / old family business / world)

5. _____

   (countries with / low income tax / world / Bahrain and Qatar)

B Match the sentences in **2A** with the comments below. Write the sentence numbers.

a. He is the co-founder of Apple Computer Inc. His salary is only $1 per year but in 2000 he received ten million stock options and a plane for staying with the company. ___
b. The income tax rate in these countries is zero because the oil industry provides the government with all its revenues. ___
c. It started in 717 AD and has been a family business for forty-six generations. ___
d. He is the head of Berkshire Hathaway. His investments come to about $28 billion. ___
e. He is the founder of Computer Associates International. His salary is about $650 million. ___

Speaking

A Find the information and complete the chart.

In your country	Name	Comment
Richest man		
Richest woman		
Largest company		
Largest bank		

B (Track 22) Answer the questions aloud.

> Who's the richest man in your country?

Messages

1 Vocabulary Business activities

A Where do people typically carry out the activities on the list? Complete the word map. (More than one answer is possible.)
(Help: Listen to the pronunciation on your audio CD. Track 23.)

call somebody
enter data
give a presentation
hold a training session
interview somebody
leave a message
make an appointment
organize a filing cabinet
process orders
reply to e-mail messages
sign a contract ✓
take a course

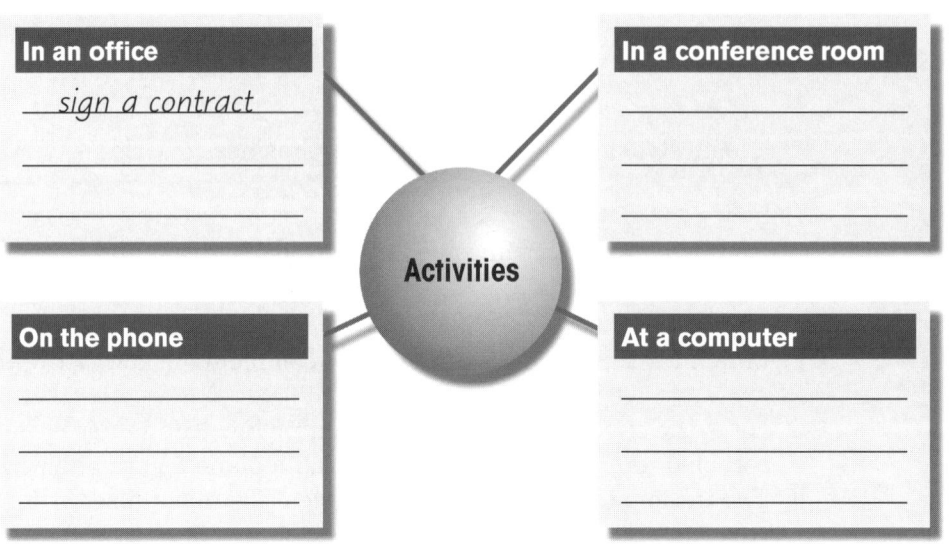

In an office
sign a contract
_____
_____

In a conference room
_____
_____

Activities

On the phone
_____
_____
_____

At a computer
_____
_____
_____

B Write about two activities you are going to do in the near future. Use the phrases above.

1. *I'm going to sign a contract with Dalton Computers.*

2. _____

3. _____

2 Listening

(Track 24) Listen to two telephone calls and write down the messages.

WHILE YOU WERE OUT

Date: _____
To: _____
From: _____
Phone: _____
Message: _____
_____
_____

WHILE YOU WERE OUT

Date: _____
To: _____
From: _____
Phone: _____
Message: _____
_____
_____

Answer key and audio scripts: page 45

Language Practice *Tell and ask*

(Help: Student's Book page 95.)

A Complete Rodney Silva's e-mail to Bob Kent, Jr. Use the words in the box.

☑ ask *or* tell ☐ that ☐ to ☐ to ☐ tell

	Form for placing orders		
File Edit View Insert Format Tools Message Help			
Send Cut Copy Paste Undo Attachment			
From	Rodney Silva		
Date	Monday, September 25th		
To	Bob Kent, Jr.		
Subject	Form for placing orders		

Dear Bob,

I have developed a new form for customers to place their orders. Could you

please __ask / tell__ your sales representatives _____ contact me about

this? I would like to explain the form _____ them. Also, could you

_____ them _____ we're going to start using the form officially next

Monday? By the way, do you have any comments on the new form?

Please let me know.

Many thanks,

Rodney Silva

B Complete the messages Rodney Silva left on the marketing assistant's desk. Use
tell or *ask*. (In some cases, both answers are possible.)

1
Could you please _____ all the
other sales representatives that we're having
a training session on Friday?

2
Could you call Mr. Grant and
_____ him if he can give a
presentation on selling techniques on Friday?

3
Would you please _____ Frank
Roach to interview the candidates for the
new sales representative position?

4
Please _____ the computer
operator to enter the new data I brought
from the last trip.

4 **Writing** *An e-mail message*

(Help: Tell and ask. Student's Book page 95.)

In your notebook, write an e-mail to a colleague asking him to pass on some messages to
other colleagues. Use the e-mail in **3A** as a model.

16 Future business

1 Reading

A What do you know about Bill Gates, Julia Roberts, and Carlos Slim Helú? In your notebook, make notes.

SUCCESS STORIES

Bill Gates

William Henry Gates III was born in Seattle in 1955. The grandson of a successful Seattle banker, Bill Gates received his first million dollars from his grandfather when he was still in college. His parents were also successful. Bill Gates's father was a lawyer and his mother a bank executive. Bill Gates's career in the world of computers started in 1975 when he dropped out of Harvard University to spend his time writing computer programs. Not long after that, he went into partnership with his friend Paul Allen, co-founded Microsoft, and started his software empire. Despite losing an antitrust ruling in 2000, Bill Gates intends to expand his empire even further, developing new software programs in the next few years.

Julia Roberts

Julie Fiona Roberts - Julia Roberts - was born in Smyrna, Georgia, in 1967. After graduating from High School, she moved to New York and tried to start a modeling career, but was not successful. She then decided to enroll in several courses for actors. In 1988, she started her movie career with "Mystic Pizza", and became a star with the movie "Steel Magnolias" in 1989. In 2001 she won an Academy Award for "Erin Brocovich".
Julia Roberts is at the peak of her career and one of Hollywood's best-paid actors. She has also founded "Shoelace", her own production company. The star now has plans to produce some of her own films.

Carlos Slim Helú

Carlos Slim Helú, Latin America's richest man, was born in Mexico City in 1940 and made a fortune buying and reselling companies. One of his most successful deals was buying Telmex - the Mexican telephone monopoly - in 1990. In four years, his fortune reached a staggering US$4.4 billion. As a result of customer complaints about the cellular division of Telmex, however, he had to spend $1.8 billion improving services. In 1997, the Mexican government opened the telecommunications market to U.S. competitors but Slim kept his share of the market and saved his business. Recently Slim has invested in Internet provider services and the computing industry. He hopes to become an even stronger investor in these areas over the next few years.

B Read "Success Stories." Have you learned anything new about the three famous people?

C Read the text again. Complete the chart.

	A past achievement	A goal for the future
Bill Gates		
Julia Roberts		
Carlos Slim		

Answer key and audio scripts: page 45

2 Language Practice   *Verb + infinitive*

(Help: Student's Book page 101.)

A Check (✓) the phrases that express intention or wishes.

☐ I'm going to	☐ I have to	☐ I plan to
☐ I must	☐ I want to	✓ I hope to
☐ I'd like to	☐ I'd love to	☐ I need to
☐ I can	☐ I may	☐ I might

B Complete these statements so that they are true for you. Use the phrases you checked in **2A**.

1. I ____*hope to*____ be promoted.

2. I _____ have a higher salary.

3. I _____ change jobs.

4. I _____ have a new boss.

5. I _____ spend some time working in another country.

6. I _____ study for an MBA in the USA.

7. I _____ start my own business.

8. I _____ retire next year.

3 Speaking

A What are your plans for the near future? Complete the chart. Use expressions from **2A**.

Area	Your plans for the near future
Professional life	_____
Personal life	_____
Social life	_____
Your next vacation	_____

B (Track 25) Answer the questions about your plans for the future aloud.

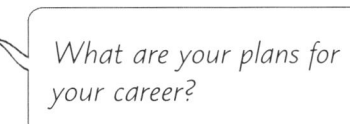

What are your plans for your career?

Word list

This list contains business terms and key vocabulary from *Business Companion 1*. To help you remember these words, space has been provided for you to write definitions, notes, or translations of these words in your native language.

(#) = unit number
adj = adjective
adv = adverb
conj = conjunction
n = noun
pp = past participle
prep = preposition
pres p = present participle
pro = pronoun
ps = simple past tense
v = verb

A

accept (3) *v* _____

according to (4) *prep* _____

accounts payable
(1) *n plural* _____

accounts receivable
(1) *n plural* _____

accounts receivable
coordinator (2) *n* _____

achievement (16) *n* _____

AD (14) *abbreviation* _____

ad (3) *n* _____

add (10) *v* _____

advantage (11) *n* _____

advice (2) *n* _____

after all (9) *prep* _____

air conditioning (4) *n* _____

all (4) *adj* _____

although (7) *conj* _____

among (5) *prep* _____

answering
machine (3) *n* _____

antitrust
ruling (16) *n* _____

anyone
else? (1) *pro adv* _____

anything
else (4) *pro adv* _____

appointment (10) *n* _____

arrival (4) *n* _____

at least (6) *adv* _____

attend (10) *v* _____

avoid (12) *v* _____

awful (12) *adj* _____

B

back trouble (12) *n* _____

bar (5) *n* _____

become (5) *v*
ps became *pp* become _____

before (4) *adv* _____

begin (5) *v*
ps began *pp* begun _____

below (3) *prep* _____

between (5) *prep* _____

blind (12) *adj* _____

board of directors (5) *n* _____

body (6) *n* _____

born, be (16) *v* _____

boss (16) *n* _____

both (15) *pro* _____

brainstorm (7) *v* _____

branch (15) *n* _____

break (12) *n* _____

bring (7) *v*
ps pp brought _____

building (11) *n* _____

built-in (3) *adj* _____

C

call (6) *n* _____

call (7) *v* _____

called (5) *adj* _____

cancel (10) *v* _____

candy (1) *n* _____

care about (9) *v prep* _____

career (16) *n* _____

careful (2) *adj* _____

carefully (9) *adv* _____

CEO (14) *abbreviation* _____

chair (8) *n* _____

check (10) *v* _____

clerk (8) *n* _____

cocktail party (2) *n* _____

coffee-maker (8) *n* _____

colleague (6) *n* _____

committed (9) *adj* _____

competent (9) *adj* _____

complaint (16) *n* _____

complex (14) *n* _____

condensed soup (5) *n* _____

conference room (8) *n* _____

construction
worker (12) *n* _____

contact (10) *v* _____

copier (3) *n* _____

copy room (8) *n* _____

cost (7) *n* _____

county (11) *n* _____

credit and
collections (1) *n* _____

cruise (4) *n* _____

customer record (10) *n* _____

customer service (1) *n* _____

D

database (10) *n* _____

deal (16) *n* _____

delegate (10) *v* _____

deluxe (4) *adj* _____

design consultant (2) *n* _____

desk (8) *n* _____

desktop (3) *adj* _____

despite (16) *prep* _____

detail (6) *n* _____

develop (5) *v* _____

director (2) *n* _____

dishonest (9) *adj* _____

disloyal (9) *adj* _____

disorganized (9) *adj* _____

drop out (16) *v adv* _____

Dutch, the (11) *n plural* _____

E

ear plugs (12) *n* _____

efficiency (6) *n* _____

empire (5) *n* _____

employee (5) *n* _____

employee profile (5) *n* _____

enjoy (4) *v* _____

enlargement (3) *n* _____

enough (3) *adj* _____

enroll (16) *v* _____

enter (11) *v* _____

enter data (15) *v n* _____

ethnic (4) *adj* _____

even further (16) *adv* _____

existing (10) *adj* _____

expand (16) *v* _____

expect (4) *v* _____

expert (2) *n* _____

extremely (9) *adv* _____

eye strain (12) *n* _____

F

facilities (4) *n* _____

fascinating (11) *adj* _____

file (10) *v* _____

filing cabinet (15) *n* _____

fill out (4) *v adv* _____

finance (1) *n* _____

financial district (11) *n* _____

find (4) *v ps pp* found _____

finding (5) *n* _____

finger (12) *n* _____

finish (6) *v* _____

fitness center (4) *n* _____

floor (1) *n* _____

floor wax (5) *n* _____

flooring business (5) *n* _____

focus (14) *v* _____

foreign exchange (14) *n* _____

forget (15) *v*

   ps forgot *pp* forgotten _____

form (15) *n* _____

found (14) *v* _____

founder (14) *n* _____

free of charge (11) *adj* _____

free time (4) *n* _____

friendly (9) *adv* _____

function (3) *n* _____

G

gender (5) *n* _____

generate (14) *v* _____

get (10) *v*

   ps got *pp* gotten _____

get in touch

   with (10) *v adv prep* _____

gigantic (14) *adj* _____

give (2) *v*

   ps gave *pp* given _____

go (4) *v ps* went *pp* gone _____

go down (7) *v adv* _____

go shopping (4) *v n* _____

go sightseeing (4) *v n* _____

go through (8) *v prep* _____

go up (7) *v adv* _____

goal (16) *n* _____

gold (11) *n* _____

gradually (11) *adv* _____

graduate (16) *v* _____

great value (3) *adj n* _____

guest (13) *n* _____

H

half (5) *n* _____

happen (7) *v* _____

hard drive (3) *n* _____

hardworking (9) *adj* _____

healthy (6) *adj* _____

hear (8) *v ps pp* heard _____

hearing loss (12) *n* _____

heavy (12) *adj* _____

helmet (12) *n* _____

help (1) *n* _____

help (1) *v* _____

high (7) *adj* _____

higher degree (5) *n* _____

hips (12) *n* _____

hold (15) *v ps pp* held _____

honest (9) *adj* _____

huge (11) *adj* _____

human resources (1) *n* _____

hurt (12) *v ps pp* hurt _____

I

I'm afraid (10) _____

ice box maker (5) *n* _____

immediately (6) *adv* _____

improve (16) *v* _____

include (5) *v* _____

income tax rate (14) *n* _____

incompetent (9) *adj* _____

increase (7) *n* _____

information

   systems (1) *n* _____

injury (12) *n* _____

insensitive (9) *adj* _____

intend (16) *v* _____

interested (7) *adj* _____

international trade

   and customs (1) *n* _____

Internet

   connection (4) *n* _____

interview (15) *v* _____

invest (16) *v* _____

investment (14) *n* _____

investor (16) *n* _____

irresponsible (9) *adj* _____

J

jar (5) *n* _____

junior/Jr. (15) *n* _____

K

kitchen (5) *n* _____

knees (12) *n* _____

L

landmark (11) *n* _____

laptop (3) *n* _____

late (9) *adj* _____

lazy (9) *adj* _____

legal size copy (3) *adj n* _____

let's see (4) _____

letter (6) *n* _____

letter size copy (3) *adj n* _____

lift (12) *v* _____

line of business (5) *n* _____

little, a (11) *adj* _____

located (8) *adj* _____

location (11) *n* _____

look forward
   to (4) *v adv prep* _____

low (7) *adj* _____

loyal (9) *adj* _____

lunch room (8) *n* _____

luxurious (11) *adj* _____

M

machine (8) *n* _____

mail room (8) *n* _____

main (10) *adj* _____

major (14) *adj* _____

make (6) *v ps pp* made _____

make sure (6) *v adj* _____

make the most
   of (6) *v superlative* _____

mall (14) *n* _____

manage (6) *v* _____

manageable (6) *adj* _____

mansion (11) *n* _____

marital status (5) *n* _____

marketing
   specialist (2) *n* _____

MBA (16) *abbreviation* _____

meeting (7) *n* _____

memory (3) *n* _____

merchant (5) *n* _____

microwave (8) *n* _____

mind (6) *n* _____

modeling career (16) *n* _____

monitor (2) *v* _____

N

neck (12) *n* _____

new (3) *adj* _____

noisy (8) *adj* _____

non-smoking (4) *adj* _____

notebook (3) *n* _____

notice (12) *n* _____

O

of course (3) *adv* _____

office (7) *n* _____

officially (15) *adv* _____

oil industry (14) *n* _____

on time (9) *adv* _____

optimistic (9) *adj* _____

order (10) *n* _____

order (13) *v* _____

order processing (1) *n* _____

organize (2) *v* _____

organized (9) *adj* _____

other (1) *adj* _____

outlet (14) *n* _____

overhead (7) *n* _____

P

packaging (1) *n* _____

page (1) *n* _____

paid (7) *see pay* _____

parking lot (14) *n* _____

partnership (16) *n* _____

pay (6) *v ps pp* paid _____

pay attention (6) *v n* _____

peak (16) *n* _____

personnel (1) *n* _____

pessimistic (9) *adj* _____

phone (6) *v* _____

phone bill (7) *n*   _____

photocopier (3) *n*   _____

place (10) *v* [an order]   _____

plan (6) *v*   _____

posture (12) *n*   _____

practically (7) *adv*   _____

preference (4) *n*   _____

pressure (12) *n*   _____

process (10) *v*   _____

production (1) *n*   _____

production costs (7) *n*   _____

production line (8) *n*   _____

production
   supervisor (2) *n*   _____

profit (7) *n*   _____

profit margin (7) *n*   _____

promote (9) *v*   _____

promotion (9) *n*   _____

provide (14) *v*   _____

public relations (1) *n*   _____

punctual (9) *adj*   _____

purchasing (1) *n*   _____

purchasing
   manager (2) *n*   _____

put (4) *v ps pp* put   _____

put up (4) *v adv*   _____

Q

quality control (1) *n*   _____

quarter (7) *n*   _____

R

rank (14) *v*   _____

reach (14) *v*   _____

ready (10) *adj*   _____

receive (7) *v*   _____

receiving (1) *n*   _____

reception (1) *n*   _____

reduce (7) *v*   _____

reduction (3) *n*   _____

relieve (12) *v*   _____

renowned (11) *adj*   _____

rent (7) *n*   _____

reply (6) *v*   _____

report (10) *n*   _____

research and
   development (1) *n*   _____

research assistant (2) *n*   _____

resell (16) *v*
   ps pp resold   _____

reservation (13) *n*   _____

resolution (3) *n*   _____

responsibility (6) *n*   _____

responsible (9) *adj*   _____

rest (4) *v*   _____

restroom (1) *n*   _____

retailer (14) *n*   _____

retire (16) *v*   _____

revenue (7) *n*   _____

river (4) *n*   _____

RSI (12) *abbreviation*   _____

ruin (12) *v*   _____

S

safe (4) *n*   _____

salary (7) *n*   _____

sales and
   marketing (1) *n*   _____

sales
   representative (2) *n*   _____

sample (8) *n*   _____

schedule (10) *v*   _____

sell (15) *v ps pp* sold   _____

send (5) *v ps pp* sent   _____

send out (8) *v adv*   _____

senior/Sr. (15) *adj*   _____

sensitive (9) *adj*   _____

several (8) *adj*   _____

share (16) *n*   _____

sheet cassette (3) *n*   _____

sheet paper
   capacity (3) *n*   _____

shelf (8) *n*
   plural shelves   _____

shipping (1) *n*   _____

shopping spree (14) *n*   _____

shot (12) n _____

show (7) v _____

showroom (8) n _____

sick (15) adj _____

sign (15) v _____

since (13) conj _____

skin cream (5) n _____

skyscraper (11) n _____

smoking (4) adj _____

socialize (13) v _____

someone (2) pro _____

sometimes (4) adv _____

soon (5) adv _____

sophisticated (3) adj _____

space (8) n _____

staff (6) n _____

staggering (16) adj _____

start (6) v _____

starting date (5) n _____

stay in (4) v adv _____

step (6) n _____

stock exchange (11) n _____

stock option (14) n _____

stockroom (8) n _____

stressful (6) adj _____

stretching
   exercise (12) n _____

subway station (8) n _____

successful (5) adj _____

such as (11) adj prep _____

suffer from (12) v prep _____

supplies (7) n plural _____

survey (5) n _____

swimming pool (4) n _____

sympathetic (9) adj _____

systems analyst (2) n _____

T

task (10) n _____

technique (15) n _____

though (9) conj _____

three-star (4) adj _____

tip (12) n _____

tossed salad (13) n _____

tour (11) n _____

training session (15) n _____

trip (4) n _____

turbine engine (14) n _____

type (12) v _____

U

uncommitted (9) adj _____

undergraduate
   degree (5) n _____

unfriendly (9) adj _____

unique (11) adj _____

unsympathetic (9) adj _____

update (10) v _____

used to (11) auxiliary _____

usually (2) adv _____

V

vacation (10) n _____

visit (2) v _____

visitor (1) n _____

visitor center (8) n _____

visitor profile (4) n _____

W

warm-up time (3) n _____

way (2) n _____

well-known (14) adj _____

win (16) v ps pp won _____

workplace (12) n _____

worried (7) adj _____

wrist (12) n _____

write (10) v
   ps wrote pp written _____

Y

You're welcome. (1) _____

Answer key

1 At a company

1 Vocabulary

A

1st floor: Customer Service / Order Processing / Packaging / Shipping
2nd floor: Accounts Payable / Accounts Receivable / Human Resources / Production

2 Listening

A

2. a / 3. d / 4. b
Audio script

Receptionist:	Can I help you?
Cindy Block:	Yes, thank you. Is Charles Connor on this floor?
Receptionist:	Yes, he is. He's in the Customer Service Department.
Cindy Block:	How about Brian Russell?
Receptionist:	Mr. Russell is in Order Processing. That's on this floor, too. Anyone else?
Cindy Block:	Yes. Jennifer Smith and Shirley Perry.
Receptionist:	Jennifer Smith is in Accounts Receivable on the second floor and... What's the name of the other person? Shirley Terry?
Cindy Block:	No, not Terry. Perry. P-E-R-R-Y.
Receptionist:	Oh, Perry. She's in Human Resources. That's on the second floor, too.
Cindy Block:	Thank you very much for your help.
Receptionist:	You're welcome!

B

2. Brian Russell is in the Order Processing Department.
3. Jennifer Smith is in the Accounts Receivable Department.
4. Shirley Perry is in the Human Resources Department.

3 Language Practice

A

2 Charles: Her name is Lisa Kim.
3 Cindy: Is she in your department?
4 Charles: No, she isn't. She's in Human Resources.
5 Cindy: Where's she from?

C

Charles:	He's
Cindy:	He's
Charles:	are / they
Cindy:	They're
Cindy:	are
Charles:	They're
Cindy:	What

2 On the job

1 Vocabulary

A

2 Director / 3 Sales Representative / 4 Research Assistant / 5 Production Supervisor / 6 Marketing Specialist / 7 Accounts Receivable Coordinator / 8 Purchasing Manager / 9 Design Consultant

B

2. consultant / 3. specialist / 4. representative / 5. assistant / 6. director / 7. coordinator, manager, supervisor (*in any order*)

2 Language Practice

A

1. Kevin: Where do you work?
   Kevin: How do you like your job?
   Nina: What do you do?
2. Nina: Where do you work?
   Nina: What do you do?
   Nina: How do you like your job?

B

1. A: does Alex Rodrigues do
2. A: does he work
3. A: Is he

3 Speaking
Audio script

Hi! I'm Nina Cortina. What's your name?
Nice to meet you.
Where are you from?
And where do you work?
What department are you in?
What do you do there?
That's interesting! How do you like your job?
Oh, there's Charles. Well, it was really nice meeting you.
Charles! Charles!

3 Buying equipment

1 Reading

A

2. b / 3. d / 4. a

B

1. 2 / 4

2 Writing

A

larger / more / than / cheaper

4 Business visitors

2 Listening

A
2. a swimming pool / a sauna
3. standard / non-smoking
4. a fax / an Internet connection
5. international food / ethnic food / vegetarian food
6. go sightseeing / stay in and rest

Audio script

Now, let's see. Number 1. Hotel accommodations...
Mmm... Of course I prefer five-star hotels. So, OK.
Question 2. Which facilities do you expect to find in your
hotel? Swimming pool, yes... Fitness center... No, I don't
want to work out... Sauna? Sauna would be great.
Sauna... yes. And I want a standard... non-smoking
room. OK. Now question 4. I don't need a safe and I
don't want air conditioning, but a fax and an Internet
connection would be great. So fax, yes... Internet
connection, yes... Now food preferences. Ha, I like all
kinds of food. International... ethnic... vegetarian.
When you have some free time on a trip, what do you
like to do? Go sightseeing? Yes. Go shopping? Mmm,
no. Hmm... I don't really like going out in the evenings
so, yes. Stay in and rest. Ok, then. That's done.

3 Language Practice

A
2. Does he like shopping?
3. Does he have any free time?
4. What does he like to do in the evenings?
5. Does he like international food?

B
A: Does he like international food?
A: Does he have any free time?
A: Does he like shopping?
A: What does he like to do in the evenings?

4 Speaking
Audio script

When you have some free time on a business trip, what
do you like do?
Do you like to go sightseeing?
How about going shopping? Do you like it?
Is there anything else you like to do when you have free
time?
And in the evenings? Do you like to go out to dinner
with colleagues or customers?
Do you like going out to see shows?
And do you sometimes like to just stay in and rest?

5 Families in business

1 Listening

B
Johnson / Lauder / Mars

Audio script

The Campbell family.
In 1869 merchant Joseph Campbell and icebox maker
Abraham Anderson form a food business called *The
Joseph A. Campbell Preserve Company.* Their most
popular product is condensed soup. Today Campbell's
Soup is almost an American icon.
The Johnson family.
Samuel Curtis Johnson buys a flooring business in
Wisconsin in 1886. This is the beginning of Johnson
Wax, one of the most famous family businesses in the
U.S. Floor wax is one of their most successful products.
The Mars family.
The Mars chocolate empire begins in 1911 when Frank
C. Mars and his wife start a candy-making operation in
their kitchen. Chocolate bars soon become their best-
selling product.
The Lauder family.
The Lauder cosmetics business starts in 1946 when
Estee Lauder's uncle develops a jar of skin cream. Now
perfumes are among their most successful products.

C

A. Family	B. Starting date	C. Line of business	D. Successful product
Campbell	1869	food	condensed soup
Johnson	1886	flooring	floor wax
Mars	1911	candy-making	chocolate bars
Lauder	1946	cosmetics	perfumes

D
2. 1886 / a flooring business. / His most successful
   product is floor wax.
3. 1911 / start a candy-making business. / Their most
   successful product is chocolate bars.
4. 1946 / starts a cosmetics business. / Their most
   successful product is perfumes.

2 Writing

A
2. Lisa Kim / 3. Thursday, July 31st /
4. An Employee Profile Survey

B
half / most / some *or* a few / many / some *or* a few /
very few / no one

6 Managing time

1 Reading

A
c When a new activity...   d Don't start a new...
f Many people never...   b Don't pay much...
e Always try to answer...

2 Language Practice

A
2. e / 3. d / 4. c / 5. a / 6. b

B
2. A: Do you ever make personal calls at work?
3. A: How well do you manage complicated activities?

4. A: Do you always try to answer letters and e-mail messages immediately?
5. A: How often do you exercise at the company gym?
6. A: How good are you at planning your day?

3 Speaking
Audio script

> Are you good at managing your time?
> Do you usually plan your day?
> And do you always answer letters and e-mail messages immediately?
> Really? And do you read the newspaper or make personal calls at work?
> Do you always finish an activity before you start another one?
> I see. So in general, are you happy with the way you manage your time?

 # 7 Company finances

1 Vocabulary
2. d / 3. f / 4. e / 5. c / 6. b / 7. a

2 Language Practice
Consultant: was
Eileen: wasn't
Eileen: were / went
Consultant: Did / go
Eileen: was

3 Reading

A
3 / 1 / 4 / 2

B
2. False / 3. True / 4. False / 5. False

 # 8 Company facilities

1 Vocabulary
2. lunch room / 3. showroom / 4. production line /
5. conference room / 6. visitor center / 7. mailroom /
8. copy room / 9. stockroom

2 Listening

A
2 / 1 / 3
Audio script

> **One.**
> I work downtown. It's not a very big place, but it's very nice. We have a small reception area. Actually, I'm the receptionist so I work there. Next to the reception area there's a big office. It's the manager's office. Across from it is a small showroom. Then there's Mr. Kent's office and across from it is the lunch room. We have a copy room, too. It's between the stockroom and Mr. Kent's office.

> **Two.**
> This is the reception area. As you can see, it's quite large. Now, if we go through this door... behind the reception area, we have the restrooms and the showroom. It's quite a big showroom. Over there, next to the showroom, we have the copy room and opposite the copy room is my office. Next to my office is the stockroom and at the very back is the lunch room.
> **Three.**
> Man: So I hear you moved to new offices.
> Woman: That's right.
> Man: Is it a nice place?
> Woman: I think so and it's bigger than the old place. We have a stockroom at the back...
> Man: Is it large?
> Woman: Oh, yes. There's lots of room. Then, next to the stockroom there is a big copy room.
> Man: How about your office?
> Woman: It's quite nice. It's between the copy room and my partner's office.
> Man: And do you have a showroom?
> Woman: Yes, it's next to the lunch room and it's also large.
> Man: It sounds like a very nice place.

3 Language Practice

A
2. There's a lunch room.
3. There isn't a visitor center.
4. There are two offices.
5. There aren't any conference rooms. *or* There isn't a conference room.

B
2. Is there a copy room?
3. Are there any offices?
4. How many restrooms are there?
5. How much space is there in the stockroom?

4 Speaking
Audio script

> Where is your company located?
> Oh, that's nice. Is it a big place?
> How many offices are there?
> And is there a lunch room?
> How about the neighborhood? Is it nice?
> Is there a subway station near your office?
> And are there any banks in the neighborhood?
> Are you happy with your office or would you like to move?

 # 9 Promoting staff

1 Vocabulary

A
Beginning with *i*: incompetent / irresponsible / insensitive
Beginning with *dis*: dishonest / disloyal / disorganized
Beginning with *un*: unfriendly / unsympathetic
Other: lazy / pessimistic / late

2 Listening

A

Pam Carson: responsible
Henry Crane: friendly, sensitive
Meg Trent: punctual, loyal
Audio script

John: So what do you think about Pam Carson?
Liz: She's very competent and knows her job well. (Mmm...) She's extremely responsible, too. You know, the kind of person who takes everything seriously.
John: Oh, that's an excellent quality, I think...
Liz: Mmm, sometimes she can be a bit unsympathetic, though. (Mmm...) She kind of expects everybody to be as responsible as she is.
John: Yes, I see what you mean. OK. What about Henry Crane?
Liz: Well, he's very friendly. And he really cares about his colleagues. He's a very sensitive guy.
John: Well, he should be. After all, he works in Public Relations. Any negative points?
Liz: Well, some of his colleagues have complained that he's... how shall I put it?... (Mmm...) he's not very organized and often leaves things for the last minute.
John: Mmm, that's not ideal, is it? (No.) Anyway... How about Meg Trent?
Liz: Oh, I don't know... She's not very friendly, is she?
John: I agree, but when you work in Credit and Collections you can't always be friendly. (Hmm...) And I'm sure she has other qualities.
Liz: Well, for one thing she's extremely punctual. Always on time for everything. And she's very loyal to the company, too. She's been with us for I don't know how many years...
John: Mmm, you're right. OK. Now let's have a look at Jennifer...

B
2. True / 3. False

3 Writing

A
2 / 1 / 3

 ## 10 Delegating tasks

1 Vocabulary

A
2. same / 3. different / 4. different / 5. different / 6. different / 7. different

B
1. Place, Process / 2. Contact, Get in touch with / 3. Write, File / 4. Schedule, Attend / 5. Make, Cancel / 6. Update, Add / 7. Check, Reply. *Get*, *write* and *make* are irregular.

C
1. update / 2. process / 3. check / 4. contact, make / 5. file / 6. attend

2 Language Practice

Brandon: Have you already contacted
Assistant: called / asked
Brandon: Have you had
Assistant: have also updated

3 Speaking

B
Audio script

Have you checked the e-mail?
And have you processed all the orders?
Did you add all the new customer records on Friday?
I see. How about the meeting next week? Have you contacted all the managers about it?
And the documents on my desk? Have you filed them?
And did you take my kids to the soccer game on Saturday?

 ## 11 Famous business centers

1 Reading

C
2. True / 3. True / 4. True / 5. True / 6. False

2 Language Practice

A
Debbie: You should visit the Fed.
Debbie: And you shouldn't miss the New York Stock Exchange.
Debbie: Ask for the visiting hours at your hotel.

 ## 12 Health at work

1 Listening

A
Kate: RSI (repetitive strain injury) / types many hours a day
Chris: stress / works too much
Ken: eye strain / looks at a computer screen all day
Bob: back trouble / lifts heavy things
Audio script

Sue: It's really awful, you know. I've worked in a factory for several years. It's really noisy. And now I can't hear very well.
Kate: What? You want me to type 20 pages for your project? You must be kidding! You know I type more than eight hours a day at work and you know my fingers and wrists hurt badly. And the minute I get home you ask me to type 20 pages for you? How insensitive!
Chris: I work more than 10 hours everyday, including weekends. And that is why I'm always tired and I'm always irritated. I just don't know what to do any more. I'd like to take some time off but I just can't and I... I... it's just awful!

| Ken: | Oh, just look at my eyes. They're red! It comes from looking at that monitor all day long. Do you think I'm going blind? |
| Bob: | You think being a construction worker is easy? Lifting heavy things all day every day ruins your back. I have terrible... Ouch... terrible backaches, ouch. Ah... |

B

Kate suffers from RSI because she types many hours a day.
Chris suffers from stress because he works too much.
Ken suffers from eye strain because he looks at a computer screen all day.
Bob suffers from back trouble because he lifts heavy things.

2 Language Practice

2. avoid lifting heavy things.
3. to take short breaks every hour.
4. to exercise two or three times a week.
5. to use ear plugs.

3 Writing

A

6 / 1 / 5 / 3 / 2 / 4

4 Speaking

Audio script

What do you suggest for sore muscles?
And do you think it's useful to take some vitamin C for a backache?
Yes... you're probably right. What about burns? Is it a good idea to put a burn under cold water? Or should you put some ointment on it?
Oh, I see. I've suffered from insomnia for years. Is there anything you would recommend?
That sounds like a good idea. You know, I often have sore eyes because of my insomnia. What should I do for that?
Well, thank you very much for all your suggestions.

13 Business meals

1 Listening

A

| 2. The customer | 4. The customer | 6. Kevin |
| 3. Kevin | 5. The customer | 7. The customer |

Audio script

Manager:	So how was dinner with Mr. Talbot last night?
Kevin:	Not too good.
Manager:	Why? What happened?
Kevin:	Well, I made a reservation at Iroha, the Japanese restaurant...
Manager:	(Hmm...) That's a nice place...
Kevin:	It is, but when we got there Mr. Talbot said he hates Japanese food. (Oh!) He wanted to go to a Mexican place. So I took him to Los Mariachis.
Manager:	Mmm... That's very nice, too.

Kevin:	But we had to wait an hour for a table.
Manager:	Oh no!
Kevin:	And since it was getting late I asked him about the contract. (Hmm...) He said he can't stand talking business before dinner...
Manager:	Oh dear!
Kevin:	... and he wanted to order. So we did.
Manager:	Did he enjoy the meal?
Kevin:	Oh, yes. Especially because when we were about to finish the mariachis came over to our table and invited him to sing with them!
Manager:	You're kidding!
Kevin:	He loved it and by the end of the evening he was very happy and wanted to pay for dinner.
Manager:	But you didn't let him pay, did you?
Kevin:	Of course not.
Manager:	And did you talk about the contract at all?
Kevin:	No. Mr. Talbot was too busy singing with the mariachis.

B

Possible answers:
Mr. Talbot hates Japanese food.
They had to wait an hour for a table.
Kevin was not able to talk to Mr. Talbot about the contract.

C

3 / 7

2 Language Practice

A

Waiter: What kind of salad would you like?
Waiter: Would you like anything to drink?
Waiter: How about you, sir?
Waiter: What would you like to order?
Waiter: Would you like anything else?

B

He doesn't let the guest order first.

C

2. Neither am I *or* I am. / 3. Neither do I *or* I don't mind *or* I do. / 4. So am I *or* I am, too *or* I am not. / 5. Neither can I *or* I can't stand them either *or* I don't mind. / 6. So do I *or* I do, too *or* I don't.

14 Business Superlatives

1 Reading

B

2. Indian Railways / 3. Walmart / 4. GE / 5. WE Mall / 6. Citigroup

2 Language Practice

A

2. The lowest paid CEO in the world is Steve Jobs.
3. The richest investor in the world is Warren Buffet.
4. Hoshi Ryokan in Japan is the oldest family business in the world.
5. The countries with the lowest income tax in the world are Bahrain and Qatar.

B

a. 2 / b. 5 / c. 4 / d. 3 / e. 1

3 Speaking

B

Audio script

Who's the richest man in your country?
Do you know anything else about him?
How about rich women in your country? Who's the richest woman?
What do you know about her?
And what is the largest company in your country?
And the largest bank?
Is that your bank?

15 Messages

1 Vocabulary

A

In an office: interview somebody / organize a filing cabinet
On the phone: call somebody / leave a message / make an appointment
In a conference room: give a presentation / hold a training session / take a course
At a computer: enter data / process orders / reply to e-mail messages

2 Listening

WHILE YOU WERE OUT
Date: _____
To: Bob Kent, Jr.
From: Rodney Silva
Phone: 555-0156 extension 224
Message: Reply to Mr. Silva's e-mail message as soon as possible.

WHILE YOU WERE OUT
Date: _____
To: Bob Kent, Sr.
From: Rodney Silva
Phone: 555-0156 extension 224
Message: The training session for sales representatives will be on Friday 9th.

Audio script

Receptionist: K S Software in New York. May I help you?
Rodney Silva: Hello. This is Rodney Silva from the Chicago branch.
Receptionist: Oh, hello, Mr. Silva.
Rodney Silva: I want to speak to Mr. Kent, please.
Receptionist: Do you want the senior Kent or Bob Kent, Jr.?
Rodney Silva: Oh, sorry. I'd like to speak to both, actually.
Receptionist: Well, I'm afraid Bob Kent, Jr. is out sick today.
Rodney: I see. Do you know if he'll be in tomorrow?
Receptionist: Yes, I think so. Would you like to leave a message?

Rodney Silva: Yes, please. Could you ask him to please reply to my e-mail message about placing orders as soon as possible? It's really important. If he'd like to talk to me he can call the office.
Receptionist: And that's our Chicago branch, 555-0156. Is that right?
Rodney Silva: That's correct. Extension 2-2-4. Thank you so much.
Receptionist: You're welcome!

Receptionist: Good afternoon. K S Sofware in New York. May I help you?
Rodney Silva: Oh hi! This is Rodney Silva from the Chicago branch, again. I forgot I needed to talk to Bob Kent, Sr. too!
Receptionist: Oh, I forgot, too. I'm really sorry but I'm afraid he's just left. May I take a message?
Rodney Silva: Would you please tell him that the training session for sales representatives will be on Friday 9th?
Receptionist: Train-ing-session. Fri-day-9th. OK. Would you like him to call you back?
Rodney Silva: That won't be necessary. Thank you. Bye-bye.
Receptionist: Bye.

3 Language Practice

A

to / to / tell / that

B

1. tell / 2. ask / 3. ask *or* tell / 4. ask *or* tell

16 Future business

1 Reading

C

Possible answers:
Bill Gates: co-founded Microsoft / develop new software programs
Julia Roberts: won an Oscar award in 2001 / produce her own films
Carlos Slim Helú: made a fortune buying and reselling companies / become an even stronger investor

2 Language Practice

A

I'm going to / I'd like to / I want to / I'd love to / I plan to

3 Speaking

B

Audio script

What are your plans for your career?
Really? Anything else at the professional level?
Now let's talk about your personal life. Do you have any special plans?
I see. And about your social life? Anything you'd like to change?
Finally, how about your next vacation? Have you already made plans?